JOHN BETJEMAN
UNCOLLECTED POEMS

UNCOLLECTED POEMS

John Betjeman

WITH A FOREWORD BY BEVIS HILLIER

JOHN MURRAY

© John Betjeman 1955, 1964, 1968, 1981, 1982
© Foreword, Bevis Hillier 1982

First published 1982
by John Murray (Publishers) Ltd
50 Albemarle Street, London w1x 4BD

Reprinted 1982

Printed in Great Britain by
Latimer Trend, Plymouth

British Library Cataloguing in Publication Data
Betjeman, John
Uncollected poems
I. Title
821'.912   PR603.E77
ISBN 0-7195-3969-2

Contents

Acknowledgements

Sir John Betjeman, Bevis Hillier and the publisher wish to express their gratitude to the staff of the Special Collections of the McPherson Library, University of Victoria, British Columbia, Canada, for their expert cataloguing of the Betjeman papers in their possession, and for the helpfulness with which they have made them available. In particular, they wish to thank Mr Howard Gerwing, Librarian, Mr Chris Petter, Archivist, Miss Joan Ryan, Library Assistant (Betjeman Archive) and Mr Dietrich Bertz, Library Assistant.

They are also indebted to Mr Duncan Andrews of New York for the loan of notebooks from his collection of Betjeman manuscripts, which helped to clarify a number of the texts.

Grateful acknowledgement is made to the Editors of *The London Magazine*, *New Statesman* and *The Listener*; to the Tragara Press, Edinburgh, who published 'Chelsea 1977' in *Hand and Eye*, a volume in honour of Sir Sacheverell Sitwell; and to Thames and Hudson who first printed 'To Stuart Piggott' in *Essays on Archaeology* edited by J. V. S. Megaw and presented to Stuart Piggott (1976).

The engravings are from *Emblems of the Christian Life*, illustrated by W. Harry Rogers (Griffith and Farran, *circa* 1880).

Foreword

According to a wine-lovers' legend, retailed by André Simon with appropriate scepticism, the first *spätlese* vintage was achieved by accident in the eighteenth century. Every year the Prince-Abbot of Fulda sent a messenger to Schloss Johannisberg bearing permission for the grape harvest to begin. In 1775 the messenger was late; the grapes stayed on the vine for longer than usual; and the resulting wine had richness and acidity in perfect proportions.

The late harvest of John Betjeman's poems garnered in this book is also the outcome of a happy accident. In 1976 I was authorized by Sir John to write his biography. 'You writing, Jock [Murray] publishing, should assure a modest sale in the circulating libraries among the older folk,' he wrote. In 1980 I was awarded a Leverhulme Fellowship to enable me to stay for two months in Victoria, British Columbia, and research into those of Sir John's unlisted papers which the University Library there had acquired nine years before, when he moved from Cloth Fair. I was warmly welcomed by the library staff, who had made an exemplary job of sorting and indexing the papers. Ranged along one wall were more than forty large steel file drawers filled with most of the letters that had been addressed to Betjeman from his undergraduate years at Oxford (1925–28) onwards.

I had made tape-recordings of Sir John, and for four years before I came to Victoria had been travelling about England and Ireland interviewing those who had known him. Even so, the Victoria archives were a revelation. One of the more startling letters was from an ex-IRA man who told Betjeman that when he was Press Attaché in Dublin his name had gone on an IRA death list; a gunman had been detailed to wait opposite the British Representative's office and to kill Betjeman when he emerged. Luckily he was away on mission at the time; and then one of the IRA men read his poems and concluded that he could not possibly be a spy.

I discovered from the papers the identity of 'Clemency, the General's daughter' in his shimmering poem 'Youth and Age on Beaulieu River, Hants', and learned how he had written it while convalescing from an operation which had taken place in Oxford (where he had been nursed by Mary Renault) in 1945. Another letter identified the 'Lincolnshire Church' in the poem of that title, where Betjeman came upon the Indian Christian priest:

> I thought of the heaving waters
> That bore him from sun glare harsh
> Of some Indian Anglican Mission
> To this green enormous marsh.

I also learned the name and address of the Lincolnshire bookseller who took Betjeman to that church. There were letters from the famous, including T. S. Eliot and Evelyn Waugh; and letters from the unknown, including countless would-be poets who sent Betjeman their halting or maladroit verses, to receive invariably a kind—often a far too kind—reply.

Among the papers, to my surprise and delight, I found a number of Betjeman poems that had not appeared in any of the collections of his work published by John Murray, nor in the first volume of his verse issued by Edward James in 1931. They included some childhood verses which Betjeman had laboriously copied into exercise books, proudly noting the age at which he composed each. Of the later poems, some were evidently final versions, typed out in fair copy. Others were the merest fragments, scribbled on the back of tailors' bills and other ephemera. The library kindly supplied photocopies.

With the help of his friend John Sparrow, the former Warden of All Souls, Oxford, Betjeman made a selection from the poems. John Sparrow advised the weeding out of the juvenilia and a few other poems, and suggested improvements to a number of lines. It is believed that most of the poems in the Victoria archive are unpublished. In this collection, they have been supplemented by a few other Betjeman poems which have appeared in magazines such as *The Listener*, the *New Statesman* and the *London Magazine* but have never been printed in a book.

The *spätlese* poems gathered here are vintage Betjeman. They come from most periods of his creative life, and traverse all the moods familiar to us in his already collected poems—from the poignant and deflated to the slapstick and hilarious. Often these moods interweave and coalesce: as Lytton Strachey said of Francis Bacon, 'He was no striped frieze: he

3

was shot silk.' For example, in the first poem in the book, '1940', the fearful vision of the destruction of his family in an air raid supervenes as the balding poet wallows in the bath. Perhaps the best of the satirical poems is 'Interior Decorator', in which a retired interior decorator rehearses his past triumphs. Compared with Betjeman's affectionate guying of the camp old designer, William Plomer's poem about the 'rose-red sissy half as old as time' looks like queer-bashing. We laugh at the decorator's memories of his crimes against taste—the beds he draped with Union Jacks, the corridors he stippled—but our sympathy is invited for his pathos:

> Eternal age is in his eyes;
> They watch the countless parties pass. . . .

Again, in 'The Retired Postal Clerk', every ounce of social comedy is extracted, but we are left feeling pangs for the bereaved clerk who does not like to use his Morris any more because it reminds him of jaunts to Carshalton Beeches, Chislehurst and Bromley:

> Where Mum would have her lemon juice and gin
> And I would have a half of old and brown—
> And those last months when she was really bad,
> They were the only pleasures that she had.

In an essay of praise for the poetry of T. S. Eliot (who, as 'the American master', taught him at High-gate Junior School) Betjeman wryly acknowledged that he himself was for ever doomed to be considered a 'funny man' of English verse. Yet even when he is

4

at his sunniest, there is usually an undertow of melancholy beneath the surface dazzle.

All the virtues of Betjeman are in this collection—and, it must be admitted, some of his vices too. Previous critics—John Sparrow, Philip Larkin and the late Lord Birkenhead in prefaces to collections of his verse, Auberon Waugh in *The New York Times Magazine* (January 6 1974) and John Bayley in a wayward but memorable essay in the *London Review of Books* (January 21 1980)—have suggested what seemed to them the cardinal merits of his poetry. But none of them was uncritical, indulgent or syrupy. Like Robert Bridges introducing Gerard Manley Hopkins to the world in 1918, they warned the public of their friend's eccentricities, and were severe on what they took to be his failings.

John Sparrow, in his preface of 1948, saw Betjeman as 'the painter of the particular, the recognizable landscape; his trees are not merely real trees with their roots in the earth, they are conifers with their roots in the red sand of Camberley, "feathery ash in leathery Lambourne", or forsythia in the Banbury Road.' Sir Harold Acton would agree with this judgment: in a long letter to me recalling his old friend, he calls John Betjeman 'the genius of the *genius loci*'. In the present collection, Betjeman's particularity in conveying sense of place is seen again, in the Douglas firs of Cheshire, the baskets of geraniums swinging over Henley river-gardens, the clumps of pine in 'sorry Surrey', the hydrangeas and raked gravel on the drive of a hunting family, the ilex shadows on the thatch of cottages at Dawlish.

But John Sparrow also felt that Betjeman's 'ready sensibility' could become 'a snare to its possessor'. 'Absorbed in their appreciation of Pont Street, its victims may lose sight of the beauty of St Paul's, and even persuade themselves, with a certain sense of triumph, that they derive a deeper pleasure from any Sandemanian meeting-house than from Salisbury Cathedral. . . . Oh worship the Lord in the beauty of ugliness!' He thought Betjeman was in danger of ending his days as the Laureate of the suburbs and the Gothic Revival. Well, there are worse things to end one's days as. Thanks largely to John Betjeman, we are all more appreciative of both the suburbs and the Gothic Revival than we were in 1948.

Lord Birkenhead agreed with Sparrow about the sense of place in Betjeman's poems, and added 'searching visual powers'; 'the true poet's instinct of registering impressions wherever he finds himself'; and 'great metrical skill'. But he felt that Betjeman had 'not, on the whole, succeeded as a satirist'—the prime role in which the 'funny man' interpretation casts him.

In 1971 Philip Larkin had the difficult task of introducing Betjeman's poems to an American readership—something W. H. Auden had affectionately attempted in a selection of 1947, *Slick but not Streamlined*, and Dylan Thomas had tried on a hall full of giggling bobby-soxers at the University of California in 1950. The truth is that Betjeman is almost unexportable. He is as incomprehensibly English as the Last Night at the Proms or the mysteries of 'U' and 'Non-U', of which his poem 'How to Get on in Society' stands as catechism to the bible of Nancy Mitford's

6

Noblesse Oblige. Larkin acknowledged Betjeman's immitigable Englishness, and made a virtue of it. The American readers were to note that Betjeman's poems were 'resolutely opposed to the spirit of the century in two major ways: they were insular, and they were regressive. To compare Betjeman with a real figure of the Twenties, a Harold Acton, is to see immediately what a poor figure he would have cut in the Paris of Stein and Cocteau: he was not, and never has been, a cosmopolitan.' This is true. 'Isn't abroad *awful*!' Betjeman once said to Edward James; and Sir Osbert Lancaster told me, 'When John is abroad, he has to be surrounded by friends, like a rugby-football player who has lost his shorts'.

Larkin thought that to understand Betjeman's insularity and non-cosmopolitanism, 'we have to realise that at Betjeman's heart lies not poetry but architecture'. And as Betjeman himself explained:

> I only enjoy to the full the architecture of these islands. This is not because I am deliberately insular, but because there is so much I want to know about a community, its history, its class distinctions, and its literature, when looking at its buildings, that abroad I find myself frustrated by my ignorance. Looking at places is not for me just going to the church or the castle or the 'places of interest' mentioned in the guide book, but walking along the streets and lanes as well, just as in a country house I do not like to see the state rooms only, but the passage to the billiard

7

room, where the Spy cartoons are, and the bed-rooms where I note the hair-brushes of the owner and the sort of hair-oil he uses.*

John Betjeman looks at architecture not just as large-scale works of art, but as the shells in which people live. In North Oxford, rusty bicycles leaning against a wall, or toothbrushes airing on the window-sill, signal to him the character of the occupants of mustard-coloured villas. In one of the poems in this book he muses:

> What interiors those panes suggest,
> Queen of lodgings in the warm south-west. . . .

and the notebook in which that unfinished poem is written contains his scribbled predictions of what might be found within, including 'a high-backed piano', 'Twilight Memories', 'Dawn in the Village' and

> Coloured 'Eventide' with a golden frame
> By an artist with a German name.

Betjeman has no rival in deducing the shellfish from the shell. He might echo what the great *Times* journalist, De Blowitz, said in his memoirs (1903): 'That which appeals to me, and which I am always searching for, is the soul which is concealed behind the silent immobility of things.'

* John Betjeman, *The English Town in the Last Hundred Years* (Cambridge University Press, 1956, p. 4.)

Like Philip Larkin, Auberon Waugh was also trying to explain Betjeman to an American audience—in *The New York Times Magazine*. He told them that Betjeman seemed to him 'the only English poet writing with real passion and original anger'. He saw him as 'acutely sensitive', sentenced, like Jack Point, the tragic clown of Gilbert and Sullivan's *Yeomen of the Guard,* 'to produce merry quips while his heart is breaking'. Love, hatred and sympathy with the inadequate were the 'three strong emotions running through all his best poetry'.

Waugh pointed out that Betjeman had contributed 'four or five poems to that undefinable and extremely limited anthology which every educated Englishman carries in his memory—more than any of his predecessors [as Poet Laureate] since Lord Tennyson.' (Cyril Connolly had made the same point in *The Modern Movement,* 1965, when he said that Betjeman 'is a poet whom one learns by heart, or like Tennyson, rather, one who slides by bits and pieces into the common experience of the race'.) Of earlier laureates, Alfred Austin contributed no memorable lines; Bridges, who by many is regarded as a masterly poet, is now chiefly remembered as senior public relations officer for Hopkins; Masefield might have written only two poems in his eighty-nine years, 'Cargoes' and 'Sea Fever'; and Cecil Day Lewis, though the author of many fine poems, wrote none that we feel obliged to commit to memory. Waugh concluded:

Among his fellow poets [Betjeman] is an enigma and an irrelevance, but he stands so far apart

9

from them that it is almost meaningless to discuss him in terms of the disregarded world of poetic movements, of obscure, tortured essays in self-exploration which pass for poetry in the universities and the Arts Council award committees. He appears to have missed the modernist cul-de-sac entirely. . . .

John Bayley, in the *London Review of Books*, also suggests that Betjeman is unrelated to his time: 'Betjeman's poetry is a particularly clear case of a poetry that does not contain its subject-matter. Never "of its time", it has turned itself into a separate space-time continuum in which there is nothing but the poetry.'

It is hard to resist the impression that Bayley is teasing us, and amusing himself, by advancing a sophistical debater's case—rather as Betjeman himself used to madden his hated Oxford tutor C. S. Lewis by suggesting that Lord Alfred Douglas was a greater poet than Shakespeare. For surely it is one of the great merits of Betjeman's poetry that it petrifies for ever a particular brief period in time—what for want of a better term might be called the 'Art Deco' period, the time of Betjeman's youth, already a source of precocious nostalgia to him by the 1940s. It was the time when chauffeur-driven Lagondas purred up pine-needle drives, when uncle wound up the new Victrola and marshalled the young party-goers for a foxtrot; when old poets of the 1890s were still to be sighted in the Café Royal.

And it is not only the Art Deco period that he has 'fixed' for ever. Like Noël Coward in his songs, he has been able to distil and bottle the essence of every decade he has lived through. No *zeitgeist* eludes his exorcism. In 'Executive', published in *A Nip in the Air* (1974), he hit off the abrasive, pushy, soulless young businessman of the 1960s (the kind of man Jonathan Aitken wrote about in *The Young Meteors*, 1967) as adeptly as he had satirized the 'Varsity' mashers of the 1920s:

> I am a young executive. No cuffs than mine are
> cleaner;
> I have a Slimline briefcase and I use the firm's
> Cortina.

How could Lord Birkenhead think him a failure as a satirist?

Betjeman always catches the exact tone of voice and diction of his characters, no matter from what class they come. The retired postal clerk:

> You'd think she would prefer
> A bigger place, with mother being gone.

The post-war advertising spiv of the Stafford Cripps austerity:

> And I have had my triumphs in my time:
> Do you remember 'Inspirated Lime—
> Sprinkle your roses with it, watch them grow
> To twice their size in half an hour or so'?

11

Yes, that was mine. A client came to talk
About some crates of surplus blackboard chalk
That he'd been landed with. I told him plain,
'You won't sell that as blackboard chalk again'.

The tiddly middle-class girl thanking her hostess for a
Bloomsbury ball, also *circa* 1945:

> Oh, Mrs Cecil-Samuel,
>   It's been the greatest fun;
> I'm sure that I've enjoyed it
>   Far more than anyone. . . .
> I cannot quite express myself,
>   I'm tied in lovers' knots;
> But oh! I am so sorry
>   About Carol's horrid spots.

And the upper-class 1960s Roman Catholic flirting
with fashionable ecumenism:

> This is my tenth; his name is Damien—
> Not Damien of Braganza on whose day
> My second youngest, Catherine, was born
> (Antonia Fraser is her godmama),
> But Damien after Father Damien,
> Whom Holy Church has just beatified.
> But I forget, you're not a Catholic,
> And this will seem too technical to you.

'Before the Lecture' is another masterpiece of mono-
logue: what public speaker has not been a victim of
the Secretary who insists on reading out the Minutes

and dealing with the Matters Arising before introducing him?

John Betjeman could be seen as flagrantly, flauntingly, anti-modernist: a twentieth-century poet who can write 'He order'd windows stainèd' must look anachronistic. A book by an American professor, Samuel Hynes's *The Auden Generation* (1976), contains not a single reference to Betjeman, though he was born in the same year as Auden, was a lifelong friend of Auden, and wrote poems which Auden confessed he envied. The reason for Betjeman's omission is that he was not a left-wing intellectual in the 1930s: though it deserves remark that while Auden and Isherwood, who had anathematized Fascism in the 1930s, stayed in America throughout the war, Betjeman (as the papers at Victoria show) moved heaven and earth to try to get into the armed forces and fight Hitler. But the particularity of Betjeman's verse puts him right alongside the moderns. Like them, he was sloughing off Victorian vagueness—'the lilies and languors of virtue, the roses and raptures of vice' —and expressing emotion through concrete images. (Just as artists of the same period wanted to get away from the muzzy lyricism of the Impressionists—what Leger crushingly called '*la peinture d'intention*'.)

With John Betjeman, we always know with what class, with what place, with what period we are dealing. Especially what period. Like John Betjeman, I was at Magdalen College, Oxford. My history tutor there, Mr A. J. P. Taylor, once said 'If you want to know what happened in the French Revolution, read J. M. Thompson [who had been Betjeman's favourite tutor

13

at Magdalen]; if you want to know what it was like to *be* in the French Revolution, read Carlyle.' Paraphrasing this, one might say 'If you want to know what happened in the twentieth century, read A. J. P. Taylor's volume in the *Oxford History of England*; if you want to know what it was like to *live* in the twentieth century, read the poems of John Betjeman.'

1982   BEVIS HILLIER

For Elizabeth

1940

As I lay in the bath the air was filling with bells;
Over the steam of the window, out in the sun,
From the village below came hoarsely the patriot yells
And I knew that the next World War had at last begun.
As I lay in the bath I saw things clear in my head :
Ten to one they'd not bother to bomb us here,
Ten to one that they'd make for the barracks instead—
As I lay in the bath, I certainly saw things clear.
As I started to dry, came a humming of expectation;
Was it the enemy planes or was it young Jack
And the rest of the gang who have passed in their aviation
Setting across to Berlin to make an attack?
As the water gurgled away I put on a shirt,
I put on my trousers, and parted what's left of my hair,
And the humming above increased to a roaring spurt
And a shuddering thud drove all the bells from the air,
And a shuddering thud drove ev'rything else to silence.
There wasn't a sound, there wasn't a soul in the street,
There wasn't a wall to the house, there wasn't a staircase;

17

There was only the bathroom linoleum under my feet.
I called, as I always do, I called to Penelope,
I called to the strong with the petulant call of the weak;
There lay the head and the brown eyes dizzily open,
And the mouth apart but the tongue unable to speak;
There lay the nut-shaped head that I love for ever,
The thin little neck, the turned-up nose and the charms
Of pouting lips and lashes and circling eyebrows;
But where was the body? and where were the legs and arms?
And somewhere about I must seek in the broken building,
Somewhere about they'll probably find my son.
Oh bountiful Gods of the air! Oh Science and Progress!
You great big wonderful world! Oh what have you done?

Interior Decorator

Eternal youth is in his eyes;
  Now he has freshened up his lips;
He slicks his hair and feigns surprise,
  Then glances at his fingertips.

'My dears, but yes, *of course* I know,
  Though why you think of asking *me*
I can't imagine, even though
  It rather *is* my cup of tea.

You see, my dears, I'm old—so old
  I'll *have* to give myself away—
So don't be flattering when you're told—
  But I was *sixty* yesterday.

And so, of course, I knew them *all*,
  And I was with them when they went
To Basil's marvellous *matelot* ball
  At Bedstead, somewhere down in Kent.

19

I was in decorating then,
   And Basil said the job was mine,
And, though I shouldn't say it, when
   I'd finished, it was just *divine*.

A *hideous* house, inside and out—
   And Basil's mother—well, not *quite*—
But still, I'll say for the old trout
   She paid my little bill all right.

I *stripped* the hideous painted wood,
   Stippled the corridors and halls,
And *pickled* everything I could,
   And *scumbled* nearly all the walls.

I put Red Ensigns on the seats
   And hung Blue Peters down their backs,
And on the beds, instead of sheets,
   Enormous pairs of Union Jacks.

My dears, just *everyone* was there—
   But oh, how *old* it makes me feel
When I recall that charming pair
   In *matelot* suits of *eau de nil*!

One was Kilcock, Clonbrassil's son,
  Who died in nineteen thirty-three
(God rest his soul!), the other one—
  Can you believe it—tiny *me*.

Bug Maxwell, Ropey, Rodney Park,
  Peter Beckhampton, Georges de Hem,
Maria Madeleine de Sark—
  I wonder what became of them?

Working in some department store—
  That was the last I heard of Bug.
Ropey was always such a bore,
  And didn't Rodney go to jug?

And Georges de Hem collaborated,
  So that's the last we'll hear of him!
And Pete and I, though we're related,
  Are out of touch, now he's so dim.

And what's become of poor Maria?
  Patrick, I'd like another drink.'
He gazes sadly at the fire,
  And solemnly pretends to think.

21

Eternal age is in his eyes;
    They watch the countless parties pass,
And, as the conversation dies,
    His consolation is the glass.

The Lift Man

In uniform behold me stand,
The lovely lift at my command.
   I press the button : Pop,
And down I go below the town;
The walls rise up as I go down
   And in the basement stop.

For weeks I've worked a morning shift
On this old Waygood-Otis lift.
   And goodness, don't I love
To press the knob that shuts the gate
When customers are shouting 'Wait!'
   And soar to floors above.

I see them from my iron cage,
Their faces looking up in rage,
   And then I call 'First floor!'
'Perfume and ladies' underwear!
'No sir, Up only. Use the stair.'
   And up again we soar.

The second floor for kiddie goods,
And kiddie-pantz and pixie-hoods,
  The third floor, restaurant :
And here the people always try
To find one going down, so I
  Am not the lift they want.

On the roof-garden floor alone
I wait for ages on my own
  High, high above the crowds.
O let them rage and let them ring,
For I am out of everything,
  Alone among the clouds.

[In 1956 John Betjeman wrote these lines, anony-
mously, for the late Gerard Hoffnung to recite.]

Archibald

The bear who sits above my bed
  A doleful bear he is to see;
From out his drooping pear-shaped head
  His woollen eyes look into me.
He has no mouth, but seems to say :
'They'll burn you on the Judgment Day.'

Those woollen eyes, the things they've seen;
  Those flannel ears, the things they've heard—
Among horse-chestnut fans of green,
  The fluting of an April bird,
And quarrelling downstairs until
Doors slammed at Thirty One West Hill.

The dreaded evening keyhole scratch
  Announcing some return below,
The nursery landing's lifted latch,
  The punishment to undergo—
Still I could smooth those half-moon ears
And wet that forehead with my tears.

Whatever rush to catch a train,
  Whatever joy there was to share
Of sounding sea-board, rainbowed rain,
  Or seaweed-scented Cornish air,
Sharing the laughs, you still were there,
You ugly, unrepentant bear.

When nine, I hid you in a loft
  And dared not let you share my bed;
My father would have thought me soft,
  Or so at least my mother said.
She only then our secret knew,
And thus my guilty passion grew.

The bear who sits above my bed
  More agèd now he is to see,
His woollen eyes have thinner thread,
  But still he seems to say to me,
In double-doom notes, like a knell :
'You're half a century nearer Hell.'

Self-pity shrouds me in a mist,
  And drowns me in my self-esteem.

The freckled faces I have kissed
   Float by me in a guilty dream.
The only constant, sitting there,
Patient and hairless, is a bear.

And if an analyst one day
   Of school of Adler, Jung or Freud
Should take this agèd bear away,
   Then, oh my God, the dreadful void!
Its draughty darkness could but be
Eternity, Eternity.

The Retired Postal Clerk

Since the wife died the house seems lonely-like,
  It isn't quite the same place as before;
Ron's got the garage for his motor-bike—
  I didn't want the Morris any more.

Ron's wife's the trouble. When I said to her,
  'Why don't you come and settle here with Ron?'
She flat refused. You'd think she would prefer
  A bigger place, with mother being gone.

But not a bit of it: and all she said
  Was, 'What I want's a place to call my own'—
She meant that she could wait till I was dead;
  So here I am, just living all alone.

I sold the Morris out Benhilton way—
  I couldn't keep it in this summer weather—
That empty seat beside me all the day;
  Along the roads we used to go together

Out to Carshalton Beeches for a spin

And back by Chislehurst and Bromley town,
Where Mum would have her lemon juice and gin

And I would have a half of old and brown—
And those last months when she was really bad,
They were the only pleasures that she had.

Cheshire

Infirmaries by Aston Webb
    On ev'ry hill surmount the pines;
From two miles off you still can see
    Their terra-cotta Dutch designs,
And metalled roads bisect canals,
    And both are crossed by railway lines.

And here a copse of Douglas firs
    Protects the merchant on the links;
The timbered club-house is not yet
    As mediaeval as he thinks;
For miles around the villas rise
    In hard interminable pinks.

Oh spin with me on pylon wires
    You Chester, Northwick, Knutsford chaps!
Look down on muddy empty fields
    And empty sheds and foot-worn gaps,
And pipes, and recreation grounds,
    And then content yourselves with maps.

30

Advertising Pays

I sit in Claridge's from twelve till two
And simply do what other people do—
Meeting and greeting persons of renown,
And looking through the people who are down.
But not *all*, mind you! Some, who're down today
Next week may put a good thing in my way.
I'm Christian names with several Labour peers;
As for Conservatives—they're rather dears,
And, just in case, you see—well, *just in case* . . .
I give them my attention for a space.
Over a whisky watered down with ice
I specialize in being *very nice*.

Why do I do it? Well, you see, I'm paid
By various representatives of Trade
For telling lies about the things they sell,
And writing lies about the things as well.
I understand the public, that is why
My entertainment costs are rather high:
Dining and wining is no light expense

31

If one's to know the men of influence.
As my old chief would say, Sir Wardour Street,
'Begin publicity with the *élite*;
Give them a glass or two of good champagne
And start a classy whispering campaign.
Then run your advertising in the press—
Start with the great, continue with the less.'
Sir Wardour, ah! he knew a thing or two:
He bought six hundred tons of government glue
And sold it all in tins as Irish stew.
And I have had my triumphs in my time:
Do you remember 'Inspirated Lime—
Sprinkle your roses with it, watch them grow
To twice their size in half an hour or so'?
Yes, that was mine. A client came to talk
About some crates of surplus blackboard chalk
That he'd been landed with. I told him plain,
'You won't sell that as blackboard chalk again.'
We both of us made thirty thousand clear:
The 'Inspirated' was my own idea.

   'Yoko' was mine, 'The Nectar of the Gods,
Prepared from Sterilized Laburnum Pods.'
Unluckily my client didn't know
Laburnum seeds were poisonous, and so. . . .

Well, that was *his* affair, the silly mug;
I'm given to understand he's still in jug.

Before the war, I started the campaign,
'If you can walk, why ever go by train?'
That was to sell a lot of surplus shoes—
And in the war, I faded from the news.

Well now, of course, what with Sir Stafford Cripps,
And sending things to India in ships,
There's not so much to lie about as when
I started in the game in nineteen-ten.
So now I'm saying 'Advertise the Truth!'
And cashing in on Planning and on Youth.
Youth centres, youth discussion groups, youth teams—
The coupons and the permits come in streams!

*Dumbleton Hall**
as by
HENRY WADSWORTH LONGFELLOW

Not so far from Evesham's city on a woody hillside green
Stands an ancient stonebuilt mansion—nothing modern to
be seen,
Not a farmhouse, not a homestead, only trees on either hand
Billowing like heaps of cushions on the sofa of the land.
When the bells from that old belfry, that the monks in
olden time
Built to God in sainted Evesham, hammer out the evening
chime
Still I seem to see the pilgrims wending down the
Chelt'nham road
Stopping for a friendly parley at the Cocks's old abode.
There perhaps goes William Shakespeare, he from Avon's
grassy side
In the creaking leather saddle on a morning horseback ride
Quaffing ale and eating oatcakes, countryman and poet he
Soon to be by printed pages bless'd with immortality.

* Built by Repton, 1837, in neo-Jacobean style.

There perhaps go rare Ben Jonson, Francis Beaumont,
Fletcher, Drake

Jolly, bold Elizabethans pausing there their thirsts to slake.

Writing plays and shooting arrows, courting, fighting, one
and all

Stopped, I deem, to steal some kisses from the daughter
of the Hall.

Time goes on into the present age of steam and gas and
roar;

Still there stands that stonebuilt mansion as it stood in
days of yore.

Not a window has been altered, not a sculptured corbel
head

But it looked on William Shakespeare decades, even
centuries, dead.

Those old pinnacles and turrets as in good Queen Bess's
reign

Still jut out above the creeper, still the level lawns remain,

And within, upon the staircase, tapestries still catch the
wind.

And there are tusks that Marco Polo may, perhaps, have
brought from Ind,

Quaint old lanterns light the carpets, quaint old carvings
deck the stair,

Sumptuous fabrics line the sofa such as Shakespeare used
to wear;
And the heiress of the Cocks's still retains the name of
Eyres,
With Sir Bolton standing by her still receives one on the
stairs;
Best of all his lovely daughter welcomes every author-
guest—
Newer Shakespeares, other Beaumonts with their Fletchers
come to rest:
Come to rest and to remember those romantic tales of old
That beside the blazing yule-log the Elizabethans told,
Come to steal, perhaps, some kisses just as Shakespeare
did and Drake—
Thus is kept thine ancient glory, Gothic Dumbleton,
awake.

Thoughts in a Train

No doubt she is somebody's mistress,
  With that Greta Garbo hair,
As she sits, mascara-lidded,
  In the corner seat over there.

But why, if she's somebody's mistress,
  Is she travelling up in a third?
Her luggage is leather, not plastic,
  Her jewelry rich and absurd.

'Oh I am nobody's mistress:
  The jewels I wear, you see,
Were, like this leather luggage,
  A present from Mummy to me.

'If you want to get on with the Government,
  You've got to be like it, I've heard;
So I've booked my suite in the Ritz Hotel
  And I'm travelling up in a Third.'

37

Shetland 1973

Fetlar is waiting. At its little quay
  Green seaweed stirs and ripples on the swell.
  The lone sham castle looks across at Yell,
And from the mainland hilltops you can see
Over to westward, glimmering distantly,
  The cliffs of Foula as the clouds dispel.
  Clear air, wide skies, crunch underfoot of shell—
The Viking kingdom waits what is to be.

Loud over Lerwick, seabirds wail and squawk,
  Portent of Shetland's fast approaching foes—
The briefcased oilmen with their wily talk;
  Soon we shall see, ranged all along the voes
Their hard-faced wives in ranch-type bungalows.

To the Crazy Gang

[Written to commemorate the last performance of the Crazy Gang in May 1962; John Betjeman presented copies of the poem to 'Monsewer' Eddie Gray, Jimmy Nervo, Jimmy Gold, Teddy Knox, Bud Flanagan, Charles Naughton and Jack Hylton.]

One Saturday night I sat in The London—
    The London Shoreditch—as peanuts cracked
With my tie askew and my waistcoat undone
    And sweating a lot as the house was packed.

The bar door swished when the bell was ringing
    And pipe smoke curled to the golden dome,
And Leo Dryden himself was singing
    Once more 'The Miner's Dream of Home'.

Oh, Saturday nights I've seen in plenty
    At the Bedford, Collins', South London, Met,
And I've laughed and wept since 1920
    At brilliant talent I can't forget.

But this is *the* Saturday night tremendous,
  This is the night with a parting pang,
This is the Saturday night to end us—
  We say goodbye to the Crazy Gang.

Goodbye old friends of the great tradition!
  From the serious thirties of slumps and tears
Into this age of nuclear fission
  You kept us laughing for thirty years.

Bud and Jimmy and Teddy you've done it,
  Monsewer, Charles Naughton and you, James Gold—
You've ridden a race and you've all of you won it
  And you've ended fresh as a two year old.

Goodbye old friends! and in skies above you
  Harry Tate, George Robey and Wilkie Bard
Are with us and watching—like us they love you—
  If there's clapping in heaven they're clapping hard.

Goodbye old friends! and now, Jack Hylton,
  I give you the greatest toast of all—
The toast of a rhymer, for I'm no Milton—
  But here's to London and Music Hall!

Kegans

On Paignton sands Hawaiian bands
   Play tunes across the sea
Like 'Home sweet home'; above the foam
   The Kegans call to me
As once again the Devon rain
   Upsets their picnic tea.

Black socks above gymnasium shoes,
   Grey bags above the socks
And golden sand on either hand
   And paper-littered rocks
And slot machines with Paris scenes
   And sharp electric shocks.

And bridge and golf and golf and bridge
   And travels in the car,
A large saloon with all aswoon
   From Reginald's cigar;
From three to four an A.A. tour
   And then the cinema.

We've left our hearts in Wimbledon
  Our feet are in the waves,
And when the rain comes down again
  We'll shelter in the caves,
And if we see impurity,
  Remember 'Jesus saves'.

Henley Regatta 1902

Underneath a light straw boater
In his pink Leander tie
Ev'ry ripple in the water caught the Captain in the eye.
O'er the plenitude of houseboats
Plop of punt-poles, creak of rowlocks,
Many a man of some distinction scanned the reach to
Temple Island
As a south wind fluttered by,
Till it shifted, westward drifting, strings of pennants
house-boat high,
Where unevenly the outline of the brick-warm town of
Henley
Dominated by her church tower and the sheds of
Brakspear's Brewery
Lay beneath a summer sky.
Plash of sculls! And pink of ices!
And the inn-yards full of ostlers, and the barrels running
dry,
And the baskets of geraniums
Swinging over river-gardens
Led us to the flowering heart of England's willow-cooled
July.

1930 Commercial Style

['The Regency did not produce "gems" either in architecture or anything else'—Sir Reginald Blomfield (the architect of the New Lambeth Bridge, Regent Street and Carlton House Terrace) in *The Times,* December 14, 1932.]

How nice to watch the buildings go

From Regent Street to Savile Row.

How nice to know, despite it all,

We need not grumble when they fall;

For ain't the big new Quadrant lined

With facings 'Architect-designed'?

What has it got to do with us—

Mere cranks who like to make a fuss—

Because we get a little tired

Of ancient men, howe'er inspired,

Who since the century began

Have built in Frenchified Queen-Anne?

Or just because we look askance

At England's Neo-Renaissance?

How nice to know that bare steel frame
Will soon look very much the same
As Greenwich: though three times as high—
A Christmas parcel for the sky,
All ugly function is not shown
When once it's wrapped in Portland stone.
That stucco in which Nash delighted
Is *false* and, like his times, benighted.
For how can Wren and Nash be call'd
As able as Sir Reginald?
And how could they, in their positions,
Have coped with modern changed conditions?
I hate to see the framework flanks
All bare behind the City banks;
I like to put, until it falls,
My capital in capitals.
How can we know, we carping fools,
Mysterious architectural rules?
And have we been to public schools?

Guilt

The clock is frozen in the tower,
　　The thickening fog with sooty smell
Has blanketed the motor power
　　Which turns the London streets to hell;
And footsteps with their lonely sound
Intensify the silence round.

I haven't hope. I haven't faith.
　　I live two lives and sometimes three.
The lives I live make life a death
　　For those who have to live with me.
Knowing the virtues that I lack,
I pat myself upon the back.

With breastplate of self-righteousness
　　And shoes of smugness on my feet,
Before the urge in me grows less
　　I hurry off to make retreat.
For somewhere, somewhere, burns a light
To lead me out into the night.

It glitters icy, thin and plain,
    And leads me down to Waterloo—
Into a warm electric train
    Which travels sorry Surrey through
And crystal-hung, the clumps of pine
Stand deadly still beside the line.

A Romance

'Twas at the Cecil-Samuels'
   In a sumptuous Holborn Hall,
Miss Dunlop and Diana Craig
   Went to a dinner-ball.
Soft as the heavy carpets
   Their eyes betrayed their souls,
As they gazed across the napery
   At well-selected Poles.

'Oh Captain Cecil-Samuel,
   I fear I'm dancing this
With Major Dobrezynski,
   And *he* knows how to kiss.
I like you very much indeed,
   And thank you all the same,
But I much prefer the Major
   With the long and funny name.'

Alas, the lush carnations!
    Each *most expensive* bloom
Was crushed against the Major
    As he whirled her round the room.
The chromium and the shaded lights
    They both began to spin
Like a glass of Lyons 'thirty-eight'
    Mixed in black-market gin.

'Oh Captain Cecil-Samuel,
    Miss Dunlop's very nice,
I know she'd like to dance with you,
    Her heart is made of ice.
My next fifteen are promised
    To the Pole that I adore,
But I like you very much indeed,
    As I have said before.'

The lights were switched to purple,
    The wine flowed on in waves,
And little jars of caviar
    Were handed round by slaves.
As Holborn Hall resounded
    To the throbbings of the band,

The Pole, he gave Diana Craig
    His castle and his hand.

'Oh Mrs Cecil-Samuel,
    It's been the greatest fun;
I'm sure that I've enjoyed it
    Far more than anyone . . . .
I cannot quite express myself,
    I'm tied in lovers' knots;
But oh! I am so sorry
    About Carol's horrid spots.'

'Two thousand pounds it cost me,'
    Said the Captain to his mate,
'And there's our daughter Carol
    And she hasn't made a date.
I fear we made our guest-list
    Far too wide and vague
When we asked that cold Miss Dunlop
    And that fast Diana Craig.'

Advent 1955

The Advent wind begins to stir
With sea-like sounds in our Scotch fir,
It's dark at breakfast, dark at tea,
And in between we only see
Clouds hurrying across the sky
And rain-wet roads the wind blows dry
And branches bending to the gale
Against great skies all silver-pale.
The world seems travelling into space,
And travelling at a faster pace
Than in the leisured summer weather
When we and it sit out together,
For now we feel the world spin round
On some momentous journey bound—
Journey to what? to whom? to where?
The Advent bells call out 'Prepare,
Your world is journeying to the birth
Of God made Man for us on earth.'

And how, in fact, do we prepare
For the great day that waits us there—
The twenty-fifth day of December,
The birth of Christ? For some it means
An interchange of hunting scenes
On coloured cards. And I remember
Last year I sent out twenty yards,
Laid end to end, of Christmas cards
To people that I scarcely know—
They'd sent a card to me, and so
I had to send one back. Oh dear!
Is this a form of Christmas cheer?
Or is it, which is less surprising,
My pride gone in for advertising?
The only cards that really count
Are that extremely small amount
From real friends who keep in touch
And are not rich but love us much.
Some ways indeed are very odd
By which we hail the birth of God.
We raise the price of things in shops,
We give plain boxes fancy tops
And lines which traders cannot sell
Thus parcell'd go extremely well.

We dole out bribes we call a present
To those to whom we must be pleasant
For business reasons. Our defence is
These bribes are charged against expenses
And bring relief in Income Tax.
Enough of these unworthy cracks!
'The time draws near the birth of Christ',
A present that cannot be priced
Given two thousand years ago.
Yet if God had not given so
He still would be a distant stranger
And not the Baby in the manger.

The Old Land Dog

AFTER HENRY NEWBOLT

Old General Artichoke lay bloated on his bed,
  Just like the Fighting Téméraire.
Twelve responsive daughters were gathered round his head
  And each of them was ten foot square.

Old General Artichoke he didn't want to die:
He never understood the truth and that perhaps was why
It wouldn't be correct to say he always told a lie.
  Womenfolk of England, oh beware!

'Fetch me down my rifle—it is hanging in the hall'
  Just like the Fighting Téméraire;
'Lydia, get my cartridge cases, twenty-four in all',
  And each of them is ten foot square.

'I'll tell you all in detail, girls, my every campaign
In Tuscany, Bolivia, Baluchistan and Spain;
And when I've finished telling you, I'll tell you all again;'
  Womenfolk of England, oh beware!

Old General Artichoke he's over eighty-two,
   Just like the Fighting Téméraire.
His daughters all make rush mats when they've nothing
                                                else to do,
   And each of them is ten foot square.

Now all ye pension'd army men from Tunbridge Wells to
                                                Perth,
Here's to General Artichoke, the purplest man on earth!
Give three loud cheers for Cheltenham, the city of his birth.
   Womenfolk of England, oh beware!

Before the Lecture

Secretary Forgive me if, just for a moment, I
Give out our notices. Will members please
Note that next Sunday in the Free Thought Hall
The Peascod Players will do *Everyman*.
The play lasts seven hours, but with a break
For light refreshments when we can adjourn
To the Club Cocoa Fountain. And I trust
That *everyman*—and every *woman*, too!—
Will see this quaint old-world morality.

Next week our lecturer is Putney Heath,
The celebrated publicist. He takes
A rather startling subject for his talk—
'Some aspects of the modern Cultural Drive
In Scandinavia'. Bring your Kirkegaards,
Also your Kafkas. We in Edgbaston
Are not behindhand in these matters.

                              Please
Send in your abstract art designs *at once*
To the Community Centre. And this year

The Art Committee asks me to point out
That no surrealist work will be allowed.
Last year, one lady member's canvas was
To say the least, well—*most* unfortunate—
She mayn't have been aware of this herself;
She worked, no doubt, with her subconscious
mind—
But there it was. So, if you please, this year
Pure abstract only. Thank you very much.

Lecturer   Ladies and gentlemen, I come to you
By kind permission of the D.I.A.,
The British Council, Min. of Ag. and Fish.,
The General Post Office, the L.M.S.,
The T.U.C., Unesco,
John Gloag and *Vogue*,
And Working Parties in the Board of Trade,
To tell you *how to beautify your homes.*

The Parochial Church Council

Last week a friend inquired of me,
'Oh, should I join our P.C.C.?'
I answered, rather priggishly,
'If you communicate, you can,
And want to help your clergyman.
Parochial Church Councils are
From Parish Councils different far'
I said, 'And District Councils too
Have very different things to do,
For District Councils raise the rates
And have political debates.
If one side says "Preserve the Town",
The other side says "Pull it down!"
And Parish Councils try to make
The District Council keep awake
To local practical affairs—
Like village bus-shelter repairs.
Parish and Parliament and Queen,
A mighty structure thus is seen—

Endless committees in between.
And I suppose that it occurr'd
To someone as not quite absurd
To make our Church of England be
A similar democracy.
The Church Assembly's near the top,
Where people talk until they drop;
Next come Diocesan Committees,
Like Mayor and Aldermen in cities.
The equivalent to R.D.C's
Are ruri decanal jamborees,
And at the root of all the tree
We find the homely P.C.C.
For P.C.C.'s were really made
To give your local vicar aid,
And I have always understood
That most of them are very good—
Where lay folk do what jobs they can
To help their church and clergyman.
But in small villages I've known
Of ones that make the vicar groan
And wish he could be left alone.
So just you come along with me
To a really wicked P.C.C.

'Tis evening in the village school,
And perched upon an infant's stool
The village postmistress is sitting
Glancing at us above her knitting.
Like schoolchildren—but do not laugh—
Farmers in desks too small by half;
Prim ladies, brooding for a storm
Are ranged like infants, on a form.
We read the text that hangs above
In coloured letters "GOD is LOVE".
The Vicar takes the teacher's chair,
A dreadful tenseness fills the air.
"We will begin," he says, "with prayer".
We do. It doesn't make things better.
The Vicar reads the Bishop's letter—
"Diocesan this and quota that"—
He might be talking through his hat;
It is not what they've come about.
And now the devil's jumping out
For next we have the church accounts,
And as they're read, the tension mounts.
This Vicar has been forced to be
The Treasurer of his P.C.C.,
As no one else will volunteer

60

To do the hard work needed here.
"Well, Vicar, do I understand
Last year we had six pounds in hand?"
Says Farmer Pinch who's rich and round
And lord of ninety thousand pound,
"And this year you are three pound ten
In debt—and in the red again.
Now, Vicar, that is not the way
To make a parson's business pay.
You're losing cash. It's got to stop
Or you will have to shut up shop."
The tactless Vicar answers, "Sir,
Upon the church you cast a slur:
Church is not Trade"; "Then time it were,"
Says Farmer Pinch. And now Miss Right
Who has been spoiling for a fight—
Miss Right who thinks she's very Low
And cannot bring herself to go
To services where people kneel,
Miss Right who always makes you feel
You're in the wrong, and sulks at home
And says the Vicar's paid by Rome—
Cries "If the Vicar and his pals
Spent less on Popish fal-de-lals

61

Like altar candles and such frills
Perhaps we then could pay our bills."
The fight grows furious and thicker,
And what was meant to help the Vicar—
This democratic P.C.C.—
Seems just the opposite to me.
The meeting soon is charged with hate,
And turns the Devil's advocate:
Its members do not come to church.
Admittedly you'd have to search
A lot of villages to find
A P.C.C. that's so unkind,
But everywhere, just now and then,
The Devil tempts the best of men;
So if you join your P.C.C.
Be calm and full of charity'.

The Shires

Harmonious hydrangeas were concealing
    The bandsmen from the scarlet and the frills
Of the Corbets and the Heywood-Lonsdales wheeling
    Among the Heber-Percys and the Hills.

Then every name meant pink and brown and stables,
    And household servants getting up at five,
And window-boxes, turreting and gables,
    And gardeners raking gravel on the drive.

The morning-room with sun on pens and blotter,
    For recapitulations of the ball—
'What did Cousin Celia see in such a rotter?'
    'Did Jack propose to Olive after all?'

An Ecumenical Invitation

This is my tenth; his name is Damien—
Not Damien of Braganza, on whose day
My second youngest, Catherine, was born
(Antonia Fraser is her godmamma),
But Damien after Father Damien,
Whom Holy Church has just beatified.
But I forget, you're not a Catholic,
And this will seem too technical to you.
Still, never mind, there's whisky over there,
Gin, sherry—help yourself—no, not for me.

Teresa, please take Damien away
I want to talk to Mr Betjeman.

Well, tell me what you think of the reforms.
I understand that *you* have had some too,
Isn't *The Times* improved beyond belief?*
It's so much bigger than it used to be!
I never like that term 'non-Catholic'—

---

* William Rees-Mogg, a Roman Catholic, had
become Editor of *The Times*.

The word we used to use for Anglicans,
Though several of my really greatest friends
Were once non-Catholics—take Evelyn Waugh
(God rest his soul!) and Graham Sutherland;
And quite the sweetest girl I ever knew,
A district nurse, was once a Methodist—
But oh, so happy as a Catholic now.
Now, won't you give our churches back to us?
Then you'll be Catholics too! I realise
It's somehow all mixed up with politics,
The Holy Father, though, will see to that;
What was I saying? England's heritage—
It *does* seem such a pity, doesn't it?
Those fine cathedrals crumbling to decay
Half empty, while our own, though brash and cheap,
Are always, always, crowded to the doors.

　　But still I didn't ask you here for that,
I want to speak of something near my heart—
The Catholic League of Women Journalists.
I, for my sins, am President this year
And with ecumenism in the air
I thought—you'll know the Holy Father's said
That all the Christians in the world, the rank
Outsiders, I mean those outside our ranks,

As well as Catholics, must play their part,
And that was why I thought of asking you
To give us this year's annual address.
It's quite informal, only half an hour.

The Conversion of St. Paul

[In 1955 Mrs Margaret Knight, a humanist, caused a sensation by her broadcasts on BBC radio attacking Christianity. This was composed in reply to her arguments, and it was published in *The Listener* of February 10, 1955]

Now is the time when we recall

The sharp Conversion of St. Paul.

Converted! Turned the wrong way round—

A man who seemed till then quite sound,

Keen on religion—very keen—

No-one, it seems, had ever been

So keen on persecuting those

Who said that Christ was God and chose

To die for this absurd belief

As Christ had died beside the thief.

Then in a sudden blinding light

Paul knew that Christ was God all right—

And very promptly lost his sight.

Poor Paul! They led him by the hand

He who had been so high and grand
A helpless blunderer, fasting, waiting,
Three days inside himself debating
In physical blindness : 'As it's true
That Christ is God and died for you,
Remember all the things you did
To keep His gospel message hid.
Remember how you helped them even
To throw the stones that murdered Stephen.
And do you think that you are strong
Enough to own that you were wrong?'
They must have been an awful time,
Those three long days repenting crime
Till Ananias came and Paul
Received his sight, and more than all
His former strength, and was baptised.
Saint Paul is often criticised
By modern people who're annoyed
At his conversion, saying Freud
Explains it all. But they omit
The really vital point of it,
Which isn't *how* it was achieved
But what it was that Paul believed.
He knew as certainly as we

Know you are you and I am me
That Christ was all He claimed to be.

What is conversion? Turning round
From chaos to a love profound.

And chaos too is an abyss
In which the only life is this.

Such a belief is quite all right
If you are sure like Mrs. Knight

And think morality will do
For all the ills we're subject to.

But raise your eyes and see with Paul
An explanation of it all.

Injustice, cancer's cruel pain,

All suffering that seems in vain,

The vastness of the universe,

Creatures like centipedes and worse—

All part of an enormous plan

Which mortal eyes can never scan

And out of it came God to man.

Jesus is God and came to show

The world we live in here below

Is just an antechamber where

We for His Father's house prepare.

What is conversion? Not at all
For me the experience of St. Paul,
No blinding light, a fitful glow
Is all the light of faith I know
Which sometimes goes completely out
And leaves me plunging round in doubt
Until I will myself to go
And worship in God's house below—
My parish Church—and even there
I find distractions everywhere.

What is Conversion? Turning round
To gaze upon a love profound.
For some of us see Jesus plain
And never once look back again,
And some of us have seen and known
And turned and gone away alone,
But most of us turn slow to see
The figure hanging on a tree
And stumble on and blindly grope
Upheld by intermittent hope.
God grant before we die we all
May see the light as did St. Paul.

St Mary Magdalen, Old Fish Street Hill

On winter evenings I walk alone in the City
    When cobbles glisten with wet and it's foggy and still;
I am Rector's warden here. But more's the pity
    We haven't the Charity children now to fill
Our old west gallery front. Some new committee
    Has done away with them all. I beg your pardon,
    I omitted to tell you where I am Rector's warden—
At St Mary Magdalen's church, Old Fish Street Hill.

Unfortunately, the London Conflagration
    Of sixteen sixty-six was a moment when
The Roman style in general estimation
    Was held so high that our church was rebuilt by Wren.
It is just a box with a fanciful plaster ceiling
Devoid of a vestige of genuine Christian feeling,
    And our congregation is seldom more than ten.

Woman Driver

What joy awaits you from the station yard,
    Oh lithe-limbed lovely in the ski-ing pants?
What warm upholstery will hold those thighs?
    What tasselled lanes from Surrey into Hants
Will meet the rapture of those dark brown eyes?
What pedal feel the Dolcis pressing hard?
Yours, revved-up Mini-minor all her own—
Her passion's plaything and her body's throne.

The Ballad of George R. Sims*

It's an easy game, this reviewin'—the editor sends yer a
book,

Yer puts it down on yer table and yer gives it a 'asty look,

An' then, Sir, yer writes about it as though yer 'ad read
it all through,

And if ye're a pal o' the author yer gives it a good review.

But if the author's a wrong 'un—and *some* are, as I've
'eard tell—

Or if 'e's a stranger to yer, why then yer can give him 'ell.

So what would yer 'ave me do, Sir, to humour an editor's
whims,

When I'm pally with Calder-Marshall, and never knew
George R. Sims?

It is easy for you to deride me and brush me off with a laugh

And say 'Well, the answer's potty—yer review it just
'arf and 'arf'—

* This was a verse review in the *New Statesman* (October 25,
1968) of a selection of George R. Sims' Ballads introduced by
Arthur Calder-Marshall.

For I fear I must change my tune, Sir, and pump the
bellows of praise
And say that both 'alves are good, Sir, in utterly different
ways.

I'm forgettin' my cockney lingo—for I lapse in my style
now and then
As Sims used to do in his ballads when he wrote of the
Upper Ten—
'Round in the sensuous galop the high-born maids are
swung
Clasped in the arms of *roués* whose vice is on every tongue'.

'It was Christmas Day in the workhouse' is his best known
line of all,
And this is his usual metre, which comes, as you may
recall,
Through Tennyson, Gordon, Kipling and on to the
Sergeants' Mess,
A rhythm that's made to recite in, be it mufti or evening
dress.

Now Arthur shows in his intro that George R. Sims was a
bloke

Who didn't compose his ballads as a sort of caustic joke;
He cared about social justice but he didn't aim very high
Though he knew how to lay on the sobstuff and make his
                          audience cry.

The village church on the back-drop is painted over
                          for good,
The village concerts are done for where the Young Reciter
                          stood,
The magic-lantern is broken and we laugh at the mission
                          hymns—
We laugh and we well might weep with the Ballads of
                          George R. Sims.

Civilized Woman

The women who walk down Oxford Street
Have bird-like faces and brick-like feet;
Floppity flop go 'tens' and 'elevens'
Of Eesiphit into D. H. Evans.
The women who walk down Oxford Street
Suffer a lot from nerves and heat,
But with Bovril, Tizer and Phospherine
They may all become what they might have been.
They gladly clatter with bag in hand
Out of the train from Metroland,
And gladly gape, when commerce calls,
At all the glory of plate-glass walls,
And gladly buy, till their bags are full,
'Milton' cleaner and 'Wolsey' wool,
'Shakespeare' cornflour, a 'Shelley' shirt,
'Brighto', 'Righto' and 'Moovyerdirt'.
Commerce pours on them gifts like rain;
Back in Metroland once again,
Wasn't it worth your weary feet—
The colourful bustle of Oxford Street?

To Stuart Piggott, 1975

Stuart, I sit here in a grateful haze
Recalling those spontaneous Berkshire days
In straw-thatched,

        chalk-built,

                pre-War

                        Uffington

Before the March of Progress had begun,
When all the world seemed waiting to be won,
When evening air with mignonette was scented,
And 'picture-windows' had not been invented,
When shooting foxes still was thought unsporting,
And White Horse Hill was still the place for courting,
When church was still the usual place for marriages
And carriage-lamps were only used for carriages.

How pleased your parents were in their retirement,
The garden and yourself their chief requirement.
Your father, now his teaching days were over,
Back in his native Berkshire lived in clover.

Your cheerful mother loyally concealed
Her inward hankering for Petersfield,
For Hampshire Downs were the first Downs you saw
And Heywood Sumner taught you there to draw.

Under great elms which rustled overhead
By stile and foot-bridge village pathways led
To cottage gardens heavy with the flower
Of fruit and vegetables towards your tower,
St Mary, Uffington, famed now as then
The perfect Parker's Glossary specimen
Of purest Early English, tall and pale,
—To tourists The Cathedral of the Vale,
To us the church. I'm glad that I survive
To greet you, Stuart, now you're sixty-five.

Chelsea 1977

The street is bathed in winter sunset pink,
The air is redolent of kitchen sink,
Between the dog-mess heaps I pick my way
To watch the dying embers of the day
Glow over Chelsea, crimson load on load
All Brangwynesque across the long King's Road.
Deep in myself I feel a sense of doom,
Fearful of death I trudge towards the tomb.
The earth beneath my feet is hardly soil
But outstretched chicken-netting coil on coil
Covering cables, sewage-pipes and wires
While underneath burn hell's eternal fires.
Snap, crackle! pop! the kiddiz know the sound
And Satan stokes his furnace underground.

Index of First Lines